MAD LIBS JUNIOR™

By Roger Price and Leonard Stern

PSS!
PRICE STERN SLOAN

PRICE STERN SLOAN
Published by the Penguin Group
Penguin Group (USA) Inc., 375 Hudson Street, New York, New York 10014, U.S.A.
Penguin Group (Canada), 90 Eglinton Avenue East, Suite 700, Toronto, Ontario, Canada M4P 2Y3
(a division of Pearson Penguin Canada Inc.)
Penguin Books Ltd, 80 Strand, London WC2R 0RL, England
Penguin Ireland, 25 St Stephen's Green, Dublin 2, Ireland
(a division of Penguin Books Ltd)
Penguin Group (Australia), 250 Camberwell Road, Camberwell, Victoria 3124, Australia
(a division of Pearson Australia Group Pty Ltd)
Penguin Books India Pvt Ltd, 11 Community Centre, Panchsheel Park, New Delhi – 110 017, India
Penguin Group (NZ), Cnr Airborne and Rosedale Roads, Albany, Auckland 1310, New Zealand
(a division of Pearson New Zealand Ltd)
Penguin Books (South Africa) (Pty) Ltd, 24 Sturdee Avenue, Rosebank, Johannesburg 2196, South Africa

Penguin Books Ltd, Registered Offices:
80 Strand, London WC2R 0RL, England

Mad Libs format copyright © 2006 by Price Stern Sloan.

Published by Price Stern Sloan, a division of Penguin Young Readers Group,
345 Hudson Street, New York, New York 10014.

ISBN 0-8431-2128-9

1 3 5 7 9 10 8 6 4 2

MAD LIBS JUNIOR™
INSTRUCTIONS

MAD LIBS JUNIOR™ is a game for kids who don't like games!
It can be played by one, two, three, four, or forty.

RIDICULOUSLY SIMPLE DIRECTIONS:

At the top of each page in this book, you will find four columns of words, each headed by a symbol. Each symbol represents a part of speech. The symbols are:

★   ☺   →   ?

NOUNS   ADJECTIVES   VERBS   MISC.

MAD LIBS JUNIOR™ is fun to play with friends, but you can also play it by yourself! To begin, look at the story on the page below. When you come to a blank space in the story, look at the symbol that appears underneath. Then find the same symbol on this page and pick a word that appears below the symbol. Put that word in the blank space, and cross out the word, so you don't use it again. Continue doing this throughout the story until you've filled in all the spaces. Finally, read your story aloud and laugh!

EXAMPLE:

"Good-bye!" he said, as he jumped into his _____ and _____
                                            ★   →

off with his pet _____ .
               ?

★ NOUNS	☺ ADJECTIVES	→ VERBS	? MISC.
car	curly	drove	hamster
boat	purple	~~danced~~	dog
roller skate	wet	drank	cat
taxicab	tired	twirled	~~giraffe~~
~~airplane~~	silly	swam	monkey

"Good-bye!" he said, as he jumped into his ___AIRPLANE___ and ___DANCED___
                                            ★   →

off with his pet ___GIRAFFE___ .
               ?

In case you haven't learned about the parts of speech yet, here is a quick lesson:

A **NOUN** ✦ is the name of a person, place, or thing. *Sidewalk, umbrella, bathtub,* and *roller blades* are nouns.

An **ADJECTIVE** ☺ describes a person, place, or thing. *Lumpy, soft, ugly, messy,* and *short* are adjectives.

A **VERB** ➜ is an action word. *Run, jump,* and *swim* are verbs.

MISC. ? can be any word at all. Some examples of a word that could be miscellaneous are: *nose, monkey, five,* and *blue.*

Say It Two Ways!

¡Abuela!	Grandmother!
¡Cuidado!	Be careful!
¡De nada!	You're welcome!
¡Excelente!	Excellent!
¡Fantástico!	Fantastic!
¡Gracias!	Thank you!
¡Hola!	Hello!
¡Lo hicimos!	We did it!
¡Muy bien!	Great!
¡Sí!	Yes!
¡Una fiesta!	A party!
¡Vamonos!	Let's go!

MAD LIBS JUNIOR™ is fun to play with friends, but you can also play it by yourself! To begin, look at the story on the page below. When you come to a blank space in the story, look at the symbol that appears underneath. Then find the same symbol on this page and pick a word that appears below the symbol. Put that word in the blank space, and cross out the word, so you don't use it again. Continue doing this throughout the story until you've filled in all the spaces. Finally, read your story aloud and laugh!

LET'S HELP BOOTS! PART 1

★	😊	➡	?
NOUNS	**ADJECTIVES**	**VERBS**	**MISC.**
pillow	green	sneezing	stones
noodle	fuzzy	clucking	horses
meatball	purple	barking	hats
sandwich	ticklish	chirping	cats
banana	red	squeaking	flowers
dress	slippery	quacking	shoes
shoe	wild	laughing	eggs
diaper	fast	croaking	frogs
strawberry	sticky	snoring	snails
ice cube	hairy	giggling	bats
marble	orange	roaring	dolls
raisin	pink	singing	puppies

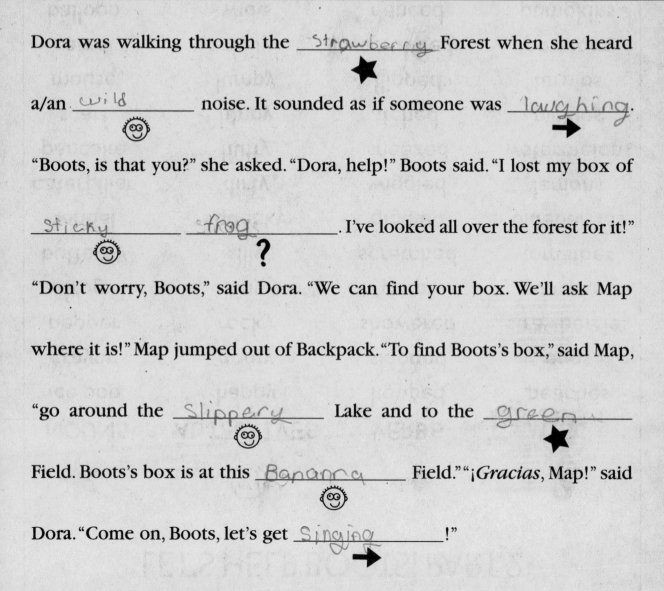

Dora was walking through the _Strawberry_ Forest when she heard

a/an _wild_ noise. It sounded as if someone was _laughing_.

"Boots, is that you?" she asked. "Dora, help!" Boots said. "I lost my box of

sticky _frog_. I've looked all over the forest for it!"

"Don't worry, Boots," said Dora. "We can find your box. We'll ask Map

where it is!" Map jumped out of Backpack. "To find Boots's box," said Map,

"go around the _Slippery_ Lake and to the _green_

Field. Boots's box is at this _Bananna_ Field." "¡Gracias, Map!" said

Dora. "Come on, Boots, let's get _singing_!"

MAD LIBS JUNIOR™ is fun to play with friends, but you can also play it by yourself! To begin, look at the story on the page below. When you come to a blank space in the story, look at the symbol that appears underneath. Then find the same symbol on this page and pick a word that appears below the symbol. Put that word in the blank space, and cross out the word, so you don't use it again. Continue doing this throughout the story until you've filled in all the spaces. Finally, read your story aloud and laugh!

LET'S HELP BOOTS! PART 2

★	😊	→	?
NOUNS	**ADJECTIVES**	**VERBS**	**MISC.**
ice pop	happy	hopped	peaches
crayon	goofy	skipped	eggs
pepper	rocky	showered	strawberries
frog	tiny	crept	cupcakes
butterfly	silly	scratched	tomatoes
sandal	squeaky	giggled	blueberries
caterpillar	dirty	wiggled	lemons
pancake	fluffy	sneezed	watermelons
scarf	funny	itched	pickles
mouse	lumpy	flipped	turnips
carrot	chilly	scrubbed	potatoes
balloon	wide	danced	pumpkins

Dora and Boots _skipped_ around the lake and soon arrived at

the field. There they found a _tiny_ _frog_ and

some _dirty_ _eggs_ under a _____

_____, but they could not find Boots's box! Boots began to feel

tired and _____, so he sat down on a _____

_____ to rest. Dora _____ on the _____

next to him. "Don't give up, Boots," she said. "We'll find your box." Suddenly,

Dora and Boots heard Benny's _____ voice. "Hi, guys," said

Benny. Dora and Boots _____ all around, but they couldn't

see the _____ bull!

MAD LIBS JUNIOR™ is fun to play with friends, but you can also play it by yourself! To begin, look at the story on the page below. When you come to a blank space in the story, look at the symbol that appears underneath. Then find the same symbol on this page and pick a word that appears below the symbol. Put that word in the blank space, and cross out the word, so you don't use it again. Continue doing this throughout the story until you've filled in all the spaces. Finally, read your story aloud and laugh!

LET'S HELP BOOTS! PART 3

★	☺	➡	?
NOUNS	**ADJECTIVES**	**VERBS**	**MISC.**
cherry	messy	whispering	bees
onion	stinky	baking	frogs
walnut	silly	whistling	puppies
cucumber	clean	singing	hummingbirds
marshmallow	chunky	cooking	horses
strawberry	wet	gobbling	fish
apple	blue	growling	ducklings
orange	sticky	sneezing	kittens
raspberry	slimy	mooing	swans
potato	sparkly	barking	penguins
lemon	pretty	fishing	cows
pear	yellow	snorting	mice

"I'm up here!" Benny shouted. Dora and Boots looked in the direction of

Benny's _____ ★. Benny was _____ ➡ under the

_____ **?** in his hot-air _____ ★. "Stay there!" Benny

shouted. "I've been _____ ➡ everywhere for you!" Dora and

Boots waited as Benny landed near a group of _____ 🙂

_____ **?**. Benny handed Boots a box. Boots peeked inside and

started _____ ➡. "It's my box! Thanks, Benny!" he exclaimed.

"But where did you find it?" Benny began _____ ➡. "A group of

_____ 🙂 _____ **?** gave it to me. They found it in the

_____ 🙂 _____ ★ Garden." "Yeah!" said Boots. "I went

_____ ➡ there yesterday!"

MAD LIBS JUNIOR™ is fun to play with friends, but you can also play it by yourself! To begin, look at the story on the page below. When you come to a blank space in the story, look at the symbol that appears underneath. Then find the same symbol on this page and pick a word that appears below the symbol. Put that word in the blank space, and cross out the word, so you don't use it again. Continue doing this throughout the story until you've filled in all the spaces. Finally, read your story aloud and laugh!

ANIMAL RESCUE

★	☺	→	?
NOUNS	**ADJECTIVES**	**VERBS**	**MISC.**
toenails	blue	pecking	chameleon
eggs	pink	buzzing	snake
crackers	long	galloping	snail
potatoes	red	skipping	frog
hats	squiggly	sliding	parrot
hammers	cheesy	swooping	dinosaur
muffins	gray	swimming	caterpillar
plums	yellow	flying	ant
pickles	frosty	chirping	grasshopper
flowers	pink	flipping	jaguar
pancakes	puffy	hopping	turtle
noses	orange	clucking	toucan

ANIMAL RESCUE

Dora, Boots, and Diego were heading to the _____ **?** Forest for a

picnic. As they passed the _____ ★ on the path, Diego stopped.

"Listen!" he whispered. "There's something _____ ➡ behind the

_____ ★ ." Suddenly, a/an _____ 😊 , _____ 😊 animal

leaped into his arms. "Do you know what it is?" Dora asked Diego. "Let's

see," Diego replied. "It has _____ 😊 eyes, a/an _____ 😊

beak, a/an _____ 😊 tail, and really _____ 😊 legs." "It

isn't a/an _____ **?** ," Dora said, "or a/an _____ **?** !" "Let's

take it to the Animal Rescue Center!" suggested Diego. "My _____ 😊

computer can tell us what it is." At the Animal Rescue Center they found

out that their new friend was a rare _____ ➡ _____ 😊

_____ **?** . "Wow!" said Diego. "I never saw this animal before!"

MAD LIBS JUNIOR™ is fun to play with friends, but you can also play it by yourself! To begin, look at the story on the page below. When you come to a blank space in the story, look at the symbol that appears underneath. Then find the same symbol on this page and pick a word that appears below the symbol. Put that word in the blank space, and cross out the word, so you don't use it again. Continue doing this throughout the story until you've filled in all the spaces. Finally, read your story aloud and laugh!

THE TREASURE MAP, PART 1

★ NOUNS	☺ ADJECTIVES	➡ VERBS	? MISC.
mittens	yellow	swimming	acorn
pencils	icy	jogging	flower
peppers	wild	fluttering	accordion
socks	furry	whistling	troll
cups	grumpy	surfing	bee
pancakes	old	popping	cymbal
stars	hairy	juggling	fly
peas	cold	humming	drum
flutes	sweet	trick-or-treating	ant
sneakers	dirty	dancing	arrow
ice skates	crispy	barking	mushroom
meatballs	short	howling	car

Dora and Boots were about to go _____ → in the _____ ☺

_____ ? Cave when Tico raced up to them in his car. *"¡Hola!"* he

said as he parked next to the _____ ★ . Tico waved a piece of

paper in the air. "Look at what Tico has," said Boots. "Let's see what's

written on it," said Dora. Boots and Tico spread the map out on a/an

_____ ? . "Hmmm," said Dora, "someone drew a gigantic

_____ ? on it. It must be a treasure map! But there's only one

way to be sure!" "Are we going _____ → ?" Boots asked. "No," said

Dora, "we're going exploring! Let's go! *¡Vamonos!*"

MAD LIBS JUNIOR™ is fun to play with friends, but you can also play it by yourself! To begin, look at the story on the page below. When you come to a blank space in the story, look at the symbol that appears underneath. Then find the same symbol on this page and pick a word that appears below the symbol. Put that word in the blank space, and cross out the word, so you don't use it again. Continue doing this throughout the story until you've filled in all the spaces. Finally, read your story aloud and laugh!

THE TREASURE MAP, PART 2

★ NOUNS	☺ ADJECTIVES	➡ VERBS	? MISC.
spiderweb	frozen	floated	carrots
anthill	purple	crawled	pancakes
flower	crunchy	bounced	eggs
rubber band	curly	boogied	acorns
muffin	fuzzy	wiggled	kiwis
hat	squeaky	twirled	onions
bean	prickly	spun	grapes
apple	fluffy	howled	limes
strawberry	hairy	skated	tomatoes
fig	fruity	flew	pretzels
mitten	gooey	barked	lemons
pinecone	rubbery	danced	potatoes

MAD LIBS JUNIOR™

THE TREASURE MAP, PART 2

The treasure map led Dora, Boots, and Tico across the _____

_____ Bridge and into the _____ _____

Tunnel. Suddenly, Tico and Boots sped up and _____ in

front of Dora. When Dora reached the end of the tunnel, all of her friends

_____ out from behind a _____ _____.

"Surprise!" they yelled. "We're the treasure!" said Benny. "It's a party for

you, Dora!" exclaimed Boots. *"¡Una fiesta!"* Tico shouted. "We made a

_____ cake for you!" Isa announced. "It has _____,

_____, and _____ icing!" "I added the _____

_____ on top!" Benny declared proudly. "It looks absolutely

_____!" Dora exclaimed. *"¡Gracias,* everyone!" *"¡De nada,*

Dora!" replied Tico.

MAD LIBS JUNIOR™ is fun to play with friends, but you can also play it by yourself! To begin, look at the story on the page below. When you come to a blank space in the story, look at the symbol that appears underneath. Then find the same symbol on this page and pick a word that appears below the symbol. Put that word in the blank space, and cross out the word, so you don't use it again. Continue doing this throughout the story until you've filled in all the spaces. Finally, read your story aloud and laugh!

FIX-IT ADVENTURE

★	☺	➡	?
NOUNS	**ADJECTIVES**	**VERBS**	**MISC.**
nose	chunky	cartwheeled	bubbles
eye	scaly	hugged	balloons
hoof	smooth	surfed	slippers
crayon	sunny	boogied	avocados
ear	bumpy	waltzed	melons
computer	salty	jumped	cabbages
spoon	sharp	screeched	leaves
pencil	slippery	pedaled	beach balls
snowflake	frosty	wiggled	pumpkins
whisker	runny	danced	buttons
peanut	green	hopped	crackers
feather	crinkly	giggled	grapes

Dora and Boots were waiting for the Big Red Chicken at the bottom of

the _____ _____ Hill. "Here he comes!" shouted

Boots. "He's riding a Big _____ Wagon!" The Big Red Chicken

_____ down the hill in his wagon so fast that he didn't even see

the pile of _____ in the road. He _____ right through

it and landed in a pit full of _____. The wagon's _____

was crushed and its _____ was crunched! The Big Red

Chicken didn't know what to do. "Don't worry!" Dora shouted. "Tool Star

can use his _____ wrench and _____ pump to fix

everything." Tool Star _____ quickly. Soon the Big Red

Chicken's wagon looked better than ever. "Thank you, Dora," he said as

he _____ away in his Big _____ Wagon.

MAD LIBS JUNIOR™ is fun to play with friends, but you can also play it by yourself! To begin, look at the story on the page below. When you come to a blank space in the story, look at the symbol that appears underneath. Then find the same symbol on this page and pick a word that appears below the symbol. Put that word in the blank space, and cross out the word, so you don't use it again. Continue doing this throughout the story until you've filled in all the spaces. Finally, read your story aloud and laugh!

THE GRUMPY OLD TROLL'S RIDDLE, PART 1

★	😊	➡	?
NOUNS	**ADJECTIVES**	**VERBS**	**MISC.**
worm	slimy	tango	candy canes
foot	silly	quack	noodles
beehive	cute	sing	pears
bus	crunchy	tumble	melons
bear	furry	hop	pickles
truck	shiny	wiggle	marshmallows
cat	plump	crawl	crumbs
ear	fluffy	whistle	cookies
cactus	young	skate	plums
caterpillar	soft	tap	eggs
tooth	thin	bounce	turnips
sock	tangy	waddle	onions

It was a warm, _____ day. Dora and Boots were heading to

the _____ _____ Park to play with their

_____. To get there, Map told them to go over the Troll Bridge

and then past the _____ _____ Mountain. The

Grumpy Old Troll stopped them as they approached the Troll Bridge.

"Cross my bridge? Not so fast. Answer this riddle before you pass," said

the Grumpy Old Troll. *"¡Excelente!"* said Dora. "We can solve any

_____ riddle," added Boots.

MAD LIBS JUNIOR™ is fun to play with friends, but you can also play it by yourself! To begin, look at the story on the page below. When you come to a blank space in the story, look at the symbol that appears underneath. Then find the same symbol on this page and pick a word that appears below the symbol. Put that word in the blank space, and cross out the word, so you don't use it again. Continue doing this throughout the story until you've filled in all the spaces. Finally, read your story aloud and laugh!

THE GRUMPY OLD TROLL'S RIDDLE, PART 2

★ NOUNS	☺ ADJECTIVES	→ VERBS	? MISC.
platypus	green	whistling	noses
porcupine	cozy	sliding	spokes
mouse	tall	hiding	fingers
zebra	spiky	sleeping	spots
toad	lovely	hopping	arms
chicken	tough	clucking	teeth
octopus	purple	crawling	ears
leopard	smelly	skipping	feathers
caterpillar	brown	dancing	beaks
rabbit	yucky	surfing	feet
pony	funny	buzzing	tongues
eel	silly	cartwheeling	toes

"Is it a/an _____ ★ ? Oh, what could it be? What has many eyes

but cannot see?" the Grumpy Old Troll asked. Dora and Boots looked

_____ 😀 as they tried to figure out the answer. Dora tapped her

_____ ? . Boots scratched his _____ ★ . They both

closed their _____ ? .Then Boots wondered, "Dora, do you think

it's a/an _____ ★ ?" "They have many _____ ? , not

eyes," Dora said. "Then maybe it is a _____ ➡ _____ ★ ,"

said Boots. "No," Dora said. "They have very _____ 😀 eyesight."

"Wait, I've got it!" said Boots.

MAD LIBS JUNIOR™ is fun to play with friends, but you can also play it by yourself! To begin, look at the story on the page below. When you come to a blank space in the story, look at the symbol that appears underneath. Then find the same symbol on this page and pick a word that appears below the symbol. Put that word in the blank space, and cross out the word, so you don't use it again. Continue doing this throughout the story until you've filled in all the spaces. Finally, read your story aloud and laugh!

THE GRUMPY OLD TROLL'S RIDDLE, PART 3

★	☺	➜	?
NOUNS	**ADJECTIVES**	**VERBS**	**MISC.**
platypus	hairy	screeching	berries
porcupine	chilly	sliding	books
mouse	prickly	singing	petunias
zebra	crunchy	snoring	tomatoes
toad	bumpy	tumbling	twigs
chicken	sleepy	squirming	leaves
octopus	moldy	rolling	acorns
leopard	stinky	whistling	beaks
cactus	yellow	tickling	sandwiches
caterpillar	sparkly	spinning	melons
rabbit	kooky	fumbling	roses
pony	spooky	cooking	drums

Boots was _____ in Dora's _____, and Dora grew

very _____—they knew the answer that would let them go

_____ over Troll Bridge. They shouted the answer: "It's a

potato! It has eyes all over, but it cannot see!" "Right!" cried the Grumpy

Old Troll, and he let them cross Troll Bridge. Dora and Boots started

_____ across. "Good job, Dora," said Boots as they passed the

_____ on the other side of Troll Bridge. "Good job, Boots,"

said Dora.

MAD LIBS JUNIOR™ is fun to play with friends, but you can also play it by yourself! To begin, look at the story on the page below. When you come to a blank space in the story, look at the symbol that appears underneath. Then find the same symbol on this page and pick a word that appears below the symbol. Put that word in the blank space, and cross out the word, so you don't use it again. Continue doing this throughout the story until you've filled in all the spaces. Finally, read your story aloud and laugh!

PUPPY'S BATH TIME

★ NOUNS	☺ ADJECTIVES	→ VERBS	? MISC.
olives	gigantic	squeezed	scooter
onions	sweet	crunched	harmonica
raisins	shiny	twisted	blanket
ice cubes	smelly	baked	dress
pineapples	fuzzy	popped	bean
cherries	rusty	flipped	pillow
strawberries	fluffy	shined	sled
noodles	green	tossed	button
bananas	sparkly	ripped	slipper
seeds	cold	giggled	dandelion
pickles	soggy	melted	meatball
watermelons	toasty	shook	mustache

PUPPY'S BATH TIME

Dora and her puppy, Perrito, were spending the day at Abuela's house.

"Perrito's fur looks very _____," said Abuela. "We should give

him a bath." *"¡Fantástico!"* said Dora. First, Dora and Abuela filled the

_____ **?** with water. They also added _____ ★ and

_____ ★ to make Perrito smell _____ .Then, Perrito

_____ ➡ into the tub, and Dora and Abuela scrubbed him with a

_____ _____ **?** . Soon, Perrito was all clean. But

before Dora and Abuela could dry him off, Perrito _____ ➡ out

of the tub and _____ ➡ his whole body. *"Cuidado,"* said Abuela.

But it was too late—Dora was soaked! "Looks like I got to take a bath, too!"

laughed Dora.

MAD LIBS JUNIOR™ is fun to play with friends, but you can also play it by yourself! To begin, look at the story on the page below. When you come to a blank space in the story, look at the symbol that appears underneath. Then find the same symbol on this page and pick a word that appears below the symbol. Put that word in the blank space, and cross out the word, so you don't use it again. Continue doing this throughout the story until you've filled in all the spaces. Finally, read your story aloud and laugh!

THE MISSING INGREDIENTS, PART 1

★	☺	→	?
NOUNS	**ADJECTIVES**	**VERBS**	**MISC.**
walnuts	mushy	boogie	cucumber
peanuts	furry	sing	grape
marshmallows	tall	tumble	pineapple
apples	crunchy	hum	radish
pinecones	gooey	whistle	pickle
pickles	thick	wiggle	watermelon
meatballs	yellow	crawl	banana
eggs	yummy	surf	tomato
cashews	big	skate	pumpkin
crackers	soft	dance	mushroom
acorns	sticky	bounce	peach
potatoes	jumbo	stretch	carrot

It was Tico's birthday, and Benny was baking a _____

cake! "I want Tico's birthday cake to be extra _____. We

need to find the sweetest ingredients for the icing!" said Benny. "That

sounds _____!" said Boots. "The sweetest _____,

_____, and _____ grow in Fairy-Tale Land," said

Dora. "Map can tell us how to get there." Map jumped out of Backpack.

"To get to Fairy-Tale Land," began Map, "_____ over the

_____ River, _____ up the _____

Beanstalk, and then you'll be there!" "Let's go!" said Dora. "One second,"

said Benny. "Let me just put the cake in the _____

to keep it _____ while we're gone."

MAD LIBS JUNIOR™ is fun to play with friends, but you can also play it by yourself! To begin, look at the story on the page below. When you come to a blank space in the story, look at the symbol that appears underneath. Then find the same symbol on this page and pick a word that appears below the symbol. Put that word in the blank space, and cross out the word, so you don't use it again. Continue doing this throughout the story until you've filled in all the spaces. Finally, read your story aloud and laugh!

THE MISSING INGREDIENTS, PART 2

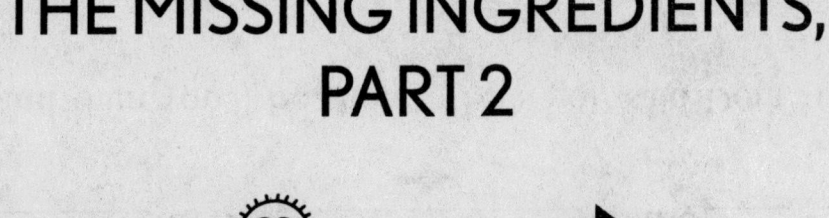

★ NOUNS	 ADJECTIVES	➡ VERBS	? MISC.
twig	pink	shining	trolls
nose	fluffy	glowing	pixies
book	stinky	spinning	elves
monkey	goofy	prancing	frogs
rainbow	droopy	somersaulting	dragons
lizard	gigantic	belly flopping	witches
lamp	purple	crawling	gumdrops
rope	squishy	trembling	bears
pumpkin	chewy	sliding	unicorns
sponge	shaky	twirling	princes
pinecone	thin	bouncing	princesses
butterfly	green	stumbling	fairies

Soon, Dora, Boots, and Benny arrived in Fairy-Tale Land. They saw

_____ _____ on a _____, _____
?   **➡**   **★**   **?**

_____ around a _____, and _____
➡   **★**   **?**

_____ over the _____! Dora, Boots, and Benny
➡   **★**

couldn't believe their eyes. They asked a group of _____
?

where they could find the _____ ingredients for Benny's
😊

icing. "All three of the ingredients grow under the _____ down
★

the path," they answered. Dora, Boots, and Benny began _____
➡

down the path. "I see the ingredients," said Dora. Benny ran ahead. "Oooh,"

he squealed. "They look so _____! Tico is going to love his
😊

_____ cake!" Back home, Tico loved his cake so much, he
😊

thanked everyone with a big *"¡Gracias!"*

MAD LIBS JUNIOR™ is fun to play with friends, but you can also play it by yourself! To begin, look at the story on the page below. When you come to a blank space in the story, look at the symbol that appears underneath. Then find the same symbol on this page and pick a word that appears below the symbol. Put that word in the blank space, and cross out the word, so you don't use it again. Continue doing this throughout the story until you've filled in all the spaces. Finally, read your story aloud and laugh!

THE FOREST FESTIVAL, PART 1

★ NOUNS	😊 ADJECTIVES	➡ VERBS	? MISC.
cucumbers	creepy	skipping	hat
porridge	silly	sliding	straw
mustard	bright	spinning	sneaker
macaroni	strange	diving	bracelet
apples	crazy	soaring	glue
peanut butter	dizzy	rolling	ice
syrup	gigantic	crawling	tiger
meatballs	slow	flipping	string
jelly	wacky	waving	feather
milk	fizzy	bouncing	foot
pancakes	yucky	squirming	jelly
beans	messy	chirping	honey

Dora and her friends were spending the day _____ →

at the Forest Festival. They were enjoying eating _____ 😊

_____ and _____ on all the rides. They had just
★ →

ridden the Ferris _____ and didn't know what to do next.
?

"Let's enter the _____ toss!" Boots said. Isa shook her
?

_____. "That's far too _____," she said. "What
★ 😊

about the tug-of-_____ contest?" Benny asked. "Too
?

_____," said Boots. "I know," said Isa. "Let's go _____
😊 →

on the roller _____!" "Great idea, Isa!" said Benny. *"Sí,"* agreed
★

Tico. "_____!" said Boots. "Come on, everyone!" said Dora.
😊

"¡Vamonos!"

MAD LIBS JUNIOR™ is fun to play with friends, but you can also play it by yourself! To begin, look at the story on the page below. When you come to a blank space in the story, look at the symbol that appears underneath. Then find the same symbol on this page and pick a word that appears below the symbol. Put that word in the blank space, and cross out the word, so you don't use it again. Continue doing this throughout the story until you've filled in all the spaces. Finally, read your story aloud and laugh!

THE FOREST FESTIVAL, PART 2

★	☺	→	?
NOUNS	**ADJECTIVES**	**VERBS**	**MISC.**
butterfly	squishy	jump	bicycles
porcupine	damp	wag	spoons
honeybee	chunky	fly	pandas
elephant	crunchy	slither	toothpicks
gerbil	tiny	chomp	robots
chicken	dirty	creep	bats
caterpillar	oily	hopscotch	buttons
leopard	green	dive	teacups
hippopotamus	yellow	bark	shirts
snake	slimy	laugh	ice cubes
grasshopper	pretty	flip	blueberries
monkey	sweaty	toss	sandwiches

Soon, Dora and her friends arrived at the roller _____.

★

It was shaped like a/an _____ with many twists and

★

_____. "Come on," said Boots. "Let's _____!"

?   ➡

Dora and her friends got in line. "Look!" said Dora. "The Fiesta Trio

is about to hand its tickets to the _____ and

★

_____ on the Roller _____." Dora

➡   ★

and her friends waved to the Fiesta Trio. "Wait!" said Dora. "That's not

a/an _____—that's Swiper. He's about to swipe the

★

Fiesta Trio's tickets!" Dora, Isa, Boots, and Benny shouted, "Swiper, no

swiping!" three times. "Oh, mannnn!" said the sneaky fox as he ran

away past the _____.

?

MAD LIBS JUNIOR™ is fun to play with friends, but you can also play it by yourself! To begin, look at the story on the page below. When you come to a blank space in the story, look at the symbol that appears underneath. Then find the same symbol on this page and pick a word that appears below the symbol. Put that word in the blank space, and cross out the word, so you don't use it again. Continue doing this throughout the story until you've filled in all the spaces. Finally, read your story aloud and laugh!

RAPID RIVERS

★ NOUNS	☺ ADJECTIVES	➡ VERBS	? MISC.
oatmeal	green	sneezing	lizard
onion	greasy	bubbling	crocodile
orange	purple	hopping	frog
marshmallow	slimy	chirping	snake
spinach	sweet	dancing	grasshopper
bean	creepy	meowing	turtle
applesauce	shiny	groaning	hyena
peanut	long	sniffing	toad
sausage	tall	snoring	gopher
ice cube	ticklish	giggling	butterfly
celery	sticky	roaring	squirrel
raisin	colorful	singing	goldfish

MAD LIBS JUNIOR
RAPID RIVERS

Dora and Boots were on their way to visit Isa. To get to her house, they

had to cross the _____ River. But every place they tried to

cross was either too _____ or too _____. "Map

will help us find a better place to cross!" Dora exclaimed. Map jumped

out of Backpack and found a bridge faster than Dora could say,

"_____ _____"! "But be quiet," Map said. "Don't

wake the _____ _____ that lives underneath it."

As Dora and Boots were crossing the bridge, Isa appeared on the other

side. She was singing a _____ song. "Shhh," whispered Boots.

"You'll wake the um . . . uh . . . the _____ _____

thing under the bridge." Isa laughed. "Don't worry about him," Isa said.

"He's a friendly _____ _____ thing."

MAD LIBS JUNIOR™ is fun to play with friends, but you can also play it by yourself! To begin, look at the story on the page below. When you come to a blank space in the story, look at the symbol that appears underneath. Then find the same symbol on this page and pick a word that appears below the symbol. Put that word in the blank space, and cross out the word, so you don't use it again. Continue doing this throughout the story until you've filled in all the spaces. Finally, read your story aloud and laugh!

OCTOPUS RESCUE, PART 1

★ 😊 ➡ **?**

NOUNS	ADJECTIVES	VERBS	MISC.
fish	furry	eating	duck
beach ball	wrinkly	skiing	eel
towel	steep	swinging	pelican
toothbrush	ugly	leaping	walrus
shovel	goofy	skating	whale
earring	rubbery	giggling	jellyfish
whisker	fluffy	hopping	clam
oar	grouchy	flying	sea horse
sandal	old	trick-or-treating	sunfish
broom	sugary	coloring	mermaid
bucket	bouncy	whispering	crab
blanket	snowy	chomping	lobster

Dora and Boots were spending the day _____ at the beach. "I

love _____ in the ocean!" Boots shouted as he rode a/an

_____ _____ to shore. "That was a really

_____ wave!" Boots said, drying his _____.

Then he hopped onto Dora's shoulders. "Let's see what else we can do at

the beach, Dora. Maybe they have a place for _____ or

_____!" Boots said excitedly. As Dora carried Boots

along the beach, she felt something tap her _____. It was

a baby octopus! "Shouldn't you be _____ in the ocean?"

Boots asked. "I was carried to shore by a/an _____

_____," the octopus replied. "Will you help me get to my

home at the bottom of the sea?" "Sure, we will," Dora said.

MAD LIBS JUNIOR™ is fun to play with friends, but you can also play it by yourself! To begin, look at the story on the page below. When you come to a blank space in the story, look at the symbol that appears underneath. Then find the same symbol on this page and pick a word that appears below the symbol. Put that word in the blank space, and cross out the word, so you don't use it again. Continue doing this throughout the story until you've filled in all the spaces. Finally, read your story aloud and laugh!

OCTOPUS RESCUE, PART 2

★ NOUNS	☺ ADJECTIVES	→ VERBS	? MISC.
snowshoes	wiggly	gargled	sea horses
helmets	slimy	flew	sea cucumbers
pants	sticky	galloped	sea scallops
shoelaces	short	shimmered	sea otters
shorts	ticklish	hopped	sea turtles
socks	dry	skipped	sea bass
scarves	wild	mooed	sea robins
mittens	long	slid	sea snakes
hats	squishy	darted	sea urchins
sneakers	tight	slithered	sea lions
binoculars	lumpy	scooted	sea monkeys
tap shoes	cuddly	stumbled	sea cows

Dora, Boots, and the baby octopus _____ into a _____

submarine and headed into the sea to find the baby octopus's home.

Dora and Boots saw many interesting creatures. _____ ?

_____, _____ _____, and

_____ _____ past the submarine. A group of

_____ wearing _____ even waved to them as

they _____ by! When they reached the baby octopus's home,

his mother _____ out to greet Dora and Boots. "Thank you for

bringing my baby home," she said. Then she wrapped her arms and arms

and arms and arms around Dora and Boots. "I like octopus hugs!" Dora

said. "They're very _____!" said Boots.

MAD LIBS JUNIOR™ is fun to play with friends, but you can also play it by yourself! To begin, look at the story on the page below. When you come to a blank space in the story, look at the symbol that appears underneath. Then find the same symbol on this page and pick a word that appears below the symbol. Put that word in the blank space, and cross out the word, so you don't use it again. Continue doing this throughout the story until you've filled in all the spaces. Finally, read your story aloud and laugh!

BENNY'S COLLECTION

★	☺	➔	?
NOUNS	**ADJECTIVES**	**VERBS**	**MISC.**
shingles	shriveled	swooped	sand dollar
sandals	sweet	slammed	sneaker
spiderwebs	sharp	skated	sugar cookie
soapsuds	salty	shimmied	sandwich
sheets	shaggy	shouted	suit
straws	soggy	screeched	shamrock
shirts	silly	scampered	shoe
sheep	shiny	snored	scarf
skateboards	spooky	smiled	shoelace
shrubs	slippery	snorted	saltshaker
shutters	shimmery	sunbathed	sprinkle
ships	sour	surfed	seashell

Today, Dora and Boots went to visit Benny at his barn. When they arrived,

the blue bull was carefully searching through his _____

_____. "¡*Hola,* Benny!" Dora said. "What are you looking for?"

"My collection of _____ _____ is gone!" Benny

said. "Maybe Swiper, that _____ fox, took them," suggested

Boots. "Maybe," replied Dora. "Or maybe they are hidden behind the

_____ _____ in the _____ cabinet."

Dora _____ over and opened the cabinet door. "There is

your collection, Benny," said Dora, pointing to a _____

filled with _____ _____. "Thanks, Dora!"

said Benny. "It wasn't the sneaky fox who put them in there—it was

_____ me!"

MAD LIBS JUNIOR™ is fun to play with friends, but you can also play it by yourself! To begin, look at the story on the page below. When you come to a blank space in the story, look at the symbol that appears underneath. Then find the same symbol on this page and pick a word that appears below the symbol. Put that word in the blank space, and cross out the word, so you don't use it again. Continue doing this throughout the story until you've filled in all the spaces. Finally, read your story aloud and laugh!

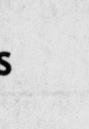

"¡Hola! This is a very special story where you can help us explore! Whenever you see this symbol ✔, write your name in the blank!"

MY EXPLORER ADVENTURE, PART 1

★ NOUNS	😃 ADJECTIVES	➡ VERBS	? MISC.
dragons	giggly	rolling	funnyfunny
lemons	chocolate	flying	sillysilly
tennis balls	twisted	galloping	wackywacky
shoelaces	tiny	sleeping	goofygoofy
crackers	vanilla	yawning	happyhappy
puppies	dry	whistling	dizzydizzy
trees	wild	mooing	zanyzany
kitties	thin	sunbathing	gigglegiggle
watermelons	squishy	gargling	smilesmile
trucks	red	humming	toothytoothy
lollipops	lumpy	shriveling	wigglewiggle
pears	hollow	drying	tickletickle

MAD LIBS JUNIOR
MY EXPLORER ADVENTURE, PART 1

Dora and Boots need to fly to the _____ planet,

_____ ?, to find a box filled with rare _____

_____ ★, and they need help. Will you help them, _____ ✓?

"¡*Gracias*, _____ ✓!" says Dora. "I'm so happy someone so

_____ can help us!" First, everyone has to prepare for their

trip. "Don't forget the _____ ★!" says Dora. "Now we have to ask

Map how to get to the planet," says Dora. "_____ ✓, say 'Map!'"

Map jumps out of Backpack. "To get to the _____ planet,"

says Map, "you must fly around the _____ → rocks that look like

_____ ★ and through the constellation of _____ ★.

Then you'll be at the planet." "*Muy bien,*" says Dora as she, Boots, and

_____ ✓ begin _____ → into the spaceship. "¡*Vamonos!*"

MAD LIBS JUNIOR™ is fun to play with friends, but you can also play it by yourself! To begin, look at the story on the page below. When you come to a blank space in the story, look at the symbol that appears underneath. Then find the same symbol on this page and pick a word that appears below the symbol. Put that word in the blank space, and cross out the word, so you don't use it again. Continue doing this throughout the story until you've filled in all the spaces. Finally, read your story aloud and laugh!

"*¡Hola!* This is a very special story where you can help us explore! Whenever you see this symbol ✔, write your name in the blank!"

MY EXPLORER ADVENTURE, PART 2

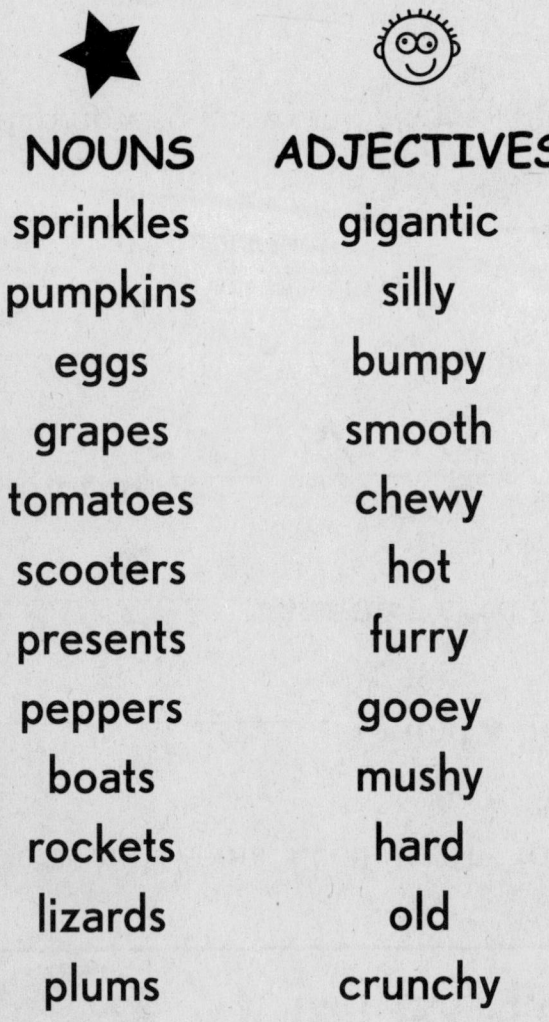

★ NOUNS	☺ ADJECTIVES	➡ VERBS	? MISC.
sprinkles	gigantic	shimmying	funnyfunny
pumpkins	silly	wiggling	sillysilly
eggs	bumpy	trotting	wackywacky
grapes	smooth	meowing	goofygoofy
tomatoes	chewy	hopping	happyhappy
scooters	hot	dancing	dizzydizzy
presents	furry	tangoing	zanyzany
peppers	gooey	mooing	gigglegiggle
boats	mushy	roaring	smilesmile
rockets	hard	lifting	toothytoothy
lizards	old	scooting	wigglewiggle
plums	crunchy	whispering	tickletickle

Now, Dora, Boots, and _____ are _____ ➡ in

space. "There are the rocks that look like _____★!" says

Dora. _____ pushes the _____★. The spaceship

starts _____ ➡ around the rocks. *¡Fantástico!* says Dora.

Next, the spaceship arrives at the constellation of _____★.

_____ grabs hold of the _____★ and steers

the spaceship through the constellation. Finally, Dora, Boots, and

_____ arrive at the planet _____? *"¡Hola!"*

Dora says to the _____★. Two little _____★

hand her a box. Dora peeks in and starts _____ ➡—it's filled

with the rare _____ _____★. *"¡Gracias!"* she

exclaims and turns to _____✓. *"¡Lo hicimos!"*

This book is published by

PSS!

PRICE STERN SLOAN

whose other splendid titles include such literary classics as

Animals, Animals, Animals! Mad Libs Junior™

Around Town Mad Libs Junior™

CANDY LAND™ Mad Libs Junior™

Halloween Mad Libs Junior™

My Little Pony™ Mad Libs Junior™

Once Upon a Mad Libs Junior™

Outer Space Mad Libs Junior™

Prehistoric Mad Libs Junior™

School Rules! Mad Libs Junior™

Scooby-Doo!™ Mad Libs Junior™

Snack Attack! Mad Libs Junior™

Sports Star Mad Libs Junior™

Summer Camp Mad Libs Junior™

Summer Fun Mad Libs Junior™

Super Silly Mad Libs Junior™

Teenage Mutant Ninja Turtles™ Mad Libs Junior™

Under the Sea Mad Libs Junior™

and many more!

Mad Libs® and Mad Libs Junior™ are available wherever books are sold.